BRAVE

The extraordinary true story of a young
woman's journey from Suicide to Freedom

TANYA CHAND

Unless otherwise stated, all scripture quotations are from the New King James Version ©

Cover Design by Narrative Studio

Photography and Illustrations by J Creation Studios

ISBN 978-0-9929897-1-2

Printed in the United Kingdom

Published by Walking Like Jesus Publishing

CONTENTS

INTRODUCTION

Looking for Love

Born in Hammersmith, West London.. I was born into rejection. My father had left before I entered the world and my mother struggled to look after me.

Growing up and not knowing him or who he was, formed a hole in my heart. A gap in which I desperately longed for my father's love. As my mother's various male friends would visit, I'd wonder if one of these men were my father. At times I reasoned that maybe some people don't have daddies. *"Daddy's little girl"* was a phrase I had heard of but never personally experienced.

I was five years old when I found out I had a father. One day whilst walking down the road, my mum asked me if I knew who my dad was. I responded *"Martin?"*, Martin was an Irish, white man who was always exceptionally nice to me and always gave me money. She laughed and said no. She told me my dad's name and that he was of Polish descent. She later then showed me photos, which she had kept as memories. Every photo was a stranger to me, I could only wonder, *"who was this man smiling back at me?"*

Not having my father left me incomplete. I always questioned whether my life would have been different, had he been a part of my life. Even if he wasn't with my mum, why couldn't he visit me at weekends? It was a complete mystery – He was a complete mystery.

My mother was born in a house (which my family still owns), within a small village in Punjab, the northern province of India. According to my grandparents, they grew concerned for my mother's wellbeing because she was an *"ill baby who could convulse at any given time"*. Therefore, my grandparents immigrated from Punjab to London in the early 1960's in search of decent healthcare. Stereotypically, they opened their own corner shop news agents and sold sweets, cigarettes and newspapers in Southall, West London.

Shortly after settling in the UK, my mum, only two at the time, was diagnosed with epilepsy; a condition of the brain which makes a person have convulsions.

My mum is one of five siblings, the second eldest. What my mum remembers of her childhood was constant admissions into hospital. She describes her childhood in one word; a 'recluse'. She wasn't very sociable and often would hide away in her room. Infamously, she became known as the *"mystery child"* because she was rarely sighted. She was insecure, embarrassed and stereotyped because of having epilepsy and being the only one of the five children to have any health concerns.

Having a disability, she considered herself the black sheep of her family. The one that something bad always happened to, which it did! She had been hit by a car at seven years old, and as a result, became deaf in one ear. On one occasion, she was fighting with her oldest sister over scissors. As they fought forwards and backwards like a tug of war, the sharp end was stabbed in my mother's eye. This narrowly missed her cornea and she barely retained her eyesight.

In her teenage years, she was heavily influenced by her parents and their culture from back home. It was customary that by seventeen years old, she would have an arranged marriage in India. Similarly, her mother was married at sixteen. To her parent's dismay, she had objected to an arranged marriage. Like any young person, she wanted to fall in love, not be forced into love. She protested and was the only one of her five siblings to do so and not get married. From then, she decided she would leave her family home. Over time, all the siblings were married off and my grandparents would then immigrate to Canada.

It was a few years following that my mother would go on to meet my father through a job they shared. From there, they would have a relationship, young and in love; just as she desired. Month's following, my mum would excitedly discover she was pregnant. My father on the other hand, unmarried and only 21 years old, nervously broke the news to his mother. She was a strong Polish woman, very religious and unhappy about the situation. In disgust, his mother was so shocked at the news, she sent my father away. She ordered him to move away, start afresh and carry on with his life.

He was forced to live in a new city and start a new life, forgetting that this pregnancy had ever happened.

That was the last time my mum would ever see him.

CHAPTER

1

The 90's Kid

I grew up in Ealing Broadway, West London in the 1990's. The Spice Girls and *"girl power"* were the anthem to my early years. I remember growing up to pick and mix penny sweets, Mr Blobby, Route master buses, the death of Princess Diana, TV's with only five channels, and the turn of the Century with the New Millennia.

My entrance into the world was dramatic. My mother nearly died from severe haemorrhaging. The trauma and upset left her unable to care for me for the first six weeks of my life. She didn't develop a bond with me and did not have much of a support network. She was too distraught with the fact my father had been made to leave and wasn't coming back. In her heart, she believed the day of my birth would be the day he would return.

Her built up hope was shattered, and depression then began. The arrival of a new baby required sudden transformation and responsibility, which she was not prepared for. I was a constant reminder of the man who broke her heart. Memories of her first love resurfaced upon my birth. For my first six weeks, I was taken in by relatives who tried to support my mother; in both an exciting but challenging time of her life.

The recollection of my early years are some feelings of loneliness and sadness. One thing I do remember growing up, was the constant reminder behind the reason my father had left. "*You're the reason why your dad left*", "*He said you'd be a problem*" my mum would say.

I was constantly blamed for my father's absence. A burden of guilt was placed upon me, resulting in further rejection. I knew it hurt my mum that she was alone. I grew up knowing I was responsible for her sadness. I knew she struggled to love me. She wasn't very affectionate or affirmative, primarily due to her own upbringing.

She suffered from depression from as early as I recall. She could lie in bed most parts of the day. I'd come home from school and the curtains would remain unopened, the house unclean. I would be left to my own devices as she would sleep most of the day. As a young girl, I was quiet and timid, but very observant.

My mother's school years were sheltered in a special needs school, and she was ignorant of the real world. Unable to establish boundaries, she could never see the bad in a person. I saw from a young age that people would take advantage of her lack of confidence and self-worth. Whether it be a spare room in the house, somewhere they could bring other friends or borrow money. They would either stay for weeks on end, steal money and jewellery and never come back again.

I remember crying myself to sleep at a young age. Wanting my mum's attention and for these ungrateful people to leave, I could see through it all. I hated the loud noise, smell of cigarettes and lack of privacy. I would read her diary entries of her friend's names and the amounts which they owed her. I would know which friends were visiting for financial gains.

Laying in my bed, I would imagine my father as a Polish Prince who would leave his castle to return to me on his horse one day. Not knowing God or even knowing if God was real; I would cry myself to sleep. Some nights, I'd talk to God. I remember one night I must have been around four or five years old and I envisioned God as this Being, in the galaxies watching over me. As I lay there weeping in the dark of night, I would ask Him to *"send me my dad"*, and if God could *"look after me."* It was the only comfort I had, as there was no one else I could, or ever would share these feelings with, to ease the pain.

Raised as an only child and being surrounded by so many adults, made me wise beyond my years. I was different to all my family. All my cousins had siblings and father's. I was the black sheep of my family. My mother was not a very affectionate person, she didn't receive much affection or affirmation in her childhood and so didn't give this to me. She rarely would hug me and tell me she loved me. Even if she did, I didn't feel she meant it, as she was so disengaged with me. Regardless of this, I wanted her time, her attention. Not having her time and attention was more hurtful. I learnt how to keep myself active and occupied, without having anyone to play with.

As the years progressed, this resulted in a very distant relationship between my mum and me. One that I could only compare to my friend's relationships and wonder, *"why I didn't have a family dynamic of a doting mother and present father?"*

From the age of 7, I practised learning to cook (with many failures), cleaning the house, taking a shopping list to the supermarket, then struggling to walk home, carrying numerous plastic bags. I vividly remember the weight of the plastic bags cutting into my young fingers and causing my fingertips to go yellow from the lack of circulation. I also learned to wake myself up and take myself to school after saying goodbye to my mum as she lay quietly in the dark. My mother would be asleep as I get up for school and would either be out or sleeping when I returned. My childhood isn't one that I look back on with active, cheerful, happy memories. Reflecting, I don't feel I had much of a 'child' hood.

With no siblings or the opportunity to be comforted and nurtured by parents, created a resilience, which made me realise I had to grow up very quickly.

Across the years, I was a good child, quite academic. My sudden maturity made me very confident from an outside perspective but not on the inside. On the inside, I was a timid girl who would always find ways to try and fit in. I'd lack any identity and ever aspire to be like the popular girls in school. Being half Polish and half Indian didn't help either, I had no friends or even role models I could relate to ethnically.

Not having a relationship with my mother, not having my dad and being an only child made me feel like I was missing out. I had friends who seemed to have lovely busy homes, thriving with life, love, comfort and security. I, on the other hand, had a dark, gloomy house with my mum who rarely interacted with me. The house was often messy, and I felt it was my responsibility to keep it maintained. I could only imagine what it would have been like if I had a dad. I spent a lot of time on my own as a young girl and would question life for myself. I began thinking more in-depth into the *'meaning of life'*, and *whether there was life after death? What was the purpose of me being here? Is this all there is to life?*

In my pursuit for answers, my desire and inquisitiveness led me to read my mother's books on spiritualism, tarot cards, dream interpretation, spirituality and horoscopes. I'd observe her, and her friends using crystals, stones and charms and be intrigued by the spiritual realm. I observed many things as she and her friends read and discussed new age books, spells, psychic's and palm readers. Often they would carry out *'spells'* in hope that my father would come back to her. In the meantime, my dream realm was becoming very active.

While my mother and her friends searched deeper into spirituality, my quest found me talking more to God; which consisted of small conversations as I go to sleep.

It was always my mum and I. Due to my mum's upbringing, she was insecure and didn't know how to love. She hadn't been to the park much as a child, so she didn't have a playful side to want to take me out for fun. My mum spent a lot of time socialising with friends at a local coffee shop, and I would sit and draw to keep myself entertained amidst adult conversation.

She would allow me to go out with my friends if they were doing activities, so that I would tag along with their family. When birthday parties came along, I would always have to find a friend who had parents that were driving, and I could go. On one occasion, my mum took me to a party but said she wouldn't be able to pick me. From the embarrassment of not having anyone to take me home, I decided to confidently make my way out of the party and pretend my mum was waiting for me up the road.

A close friend's mum noticed and asked if I had a lift home, I was honest and said I didn't. She kindly took me home. It was an embarrassing situation, but I never felt like she judged me, and my friend Hatty was unaware. Her ignorance was bliss. Hatty's mum would invite me to their house often, after school, and I would be in awe of what a busy home Hatty had; arguing siblings, her doting mum preparing food and her dad walking in removing his tie from his busy day in the office. Although, I felt out of place, the only olive-skinned girl in the house. I enjoyed being a fly on the wall, getting an insight into healthy family life.

At times my mum wasn't interested in what I was doing. If I asked her to keep me company and do an activity together, she would tell me to go and play on my own. Television dramas, gossip magazines, and friends were her focus of attention. It saddened me that she wouldn't try to spend time with me in ways I wanted. She felt that by buying me materialistic things was sufficient, I didn't want 'things', I needed time and attention. But my mum just did not know how to give those things.

Most of my friends and family had their dads who taught them how to ride a bike; they'd attach stabilisers, push them on and catch them if they fell.

Not me. I taught myself how to ride a bike in one day!

I wasn't bought a new pink tricycle with my favourite Disney character of that time like other girls. I was too outgrown for that.

One afternoon, a family friend Maggie came to visit. As she arrived, she walked to the door with a second-hand black and green bike for me! I was so happy until the thoughts crept in: "*but I don't have a daddy to teach me how to ride*". By this point, I was a very tall eight-year-old and felt silly to want stabilisers. Especially considering my height for my age, I looked as though I was ten years old. Wanting to give it a go, I pushed the bike outside, and I got on to the saddle. I peddled and I slowly saw the world turn on its axis…as I fell over and grazed my knee.

With blood dribbling down my grazed knee, I told myself not to cry; I didn't care! Determined, I got up, and I put my foot on the pedal, then the other lever. My knees begin to rise, and I'm now peddling! I was confident that I wouldn't fall off this time. I was so proud of myself, no cheer from daddy behind me, at the side-wings in case I fell.

I had done this by myself and for myself.

CHAPTER

2

This is Your Father

In 2002, I was ten years old, and my mother met a man who would soon become my step-father. I was so excited, I would now have a father of my own. A father was something I only imagined, had dreamt about, but now could be a reality. It took time adjusting, having a male presence in my life. It had only ever been my mum and me. I had to deal with my mum's focus and attention being toward a man for the first time, and this was tough. Her sudden interest in make-up and dressing up was good for her, and I enjoyed seeing her feeling good about herself. It was a first. Her sadness and depression seemed to have disappeared. She was now happy, and I finally had a father!

He would happily take me to the park to play with me, something my mother would never do. He would play games with me, watch movies and be more interactive than my mum was – I loved it.

However, after a while, I would start to realise that there was more to this man than meets the eye.

It was evident he wasn't my father, there were no resemblances. It was one day we were walking in a park, and he had a can of beer and quickly threw it into a bush; because of the police officers that were walking towards us. He went on to explain that people could think he (a white older man) was a paedophile talking with me (a young olive-skinned girl) in a park and holding a can of beer was inappropriate. *"A paedophile?"*, a thought that had never even crossed my mind, what made him think of that? I began to think I was doing something wrong. That remark made me feel somewhat uncomfortable around my mum's partner. Then after a few months, I noticed more alcohol, and especially that he would hide it. When I began to see half full cans of beer left by the garden door in the morning, I knew something was up. Given that most people enjoy a drink in the evening, I soon began to see that he was, in fact, an alcoholic. I put two and two together and questioned my mum. But she ignored me and told me not to be so silly. Then came the angry side in his drunken state, which would progress into verbal abuse. For the first time, I witnessed and experienced mistreatment towards my mother and it made me feel helpless. Gradually, the anger would be directed towards me and I would find myself defenceless. Other comments would arise as to how my body was developing in specific areas. I began to feel extremely uncomfortable, uneased and self-conscious around him. I knew his choice of words and character were inappropriate. When telling the adults around me, they laughed it off and never seemed to have an issue with it. If anything, they said I was jealous of his likening to my mum and that I wanted his attention. And this only encouraged his rude behaviour. One night I was trying to sleep, and he had left the door open intentionally and played pornography so loudly. I cried myself to sleep, screaming internally. It was torture. No one thought this was wrong and I had to put up with this. The following morning, I was so saddened and hurt, I plucked up the courage to tell my mum one last time about his actions. She was ironing at the time, and as I boldly stood there holding back the tears, I tell my mum what I experienced and how horrible it made me feel. She merely responded with an "*ok*".

"*OK*?" I screamed. I was so hurt by her lack of response. I learnt to just put up with his disturbed personality. She was too weak to put him right. So as time progressed, I began to hate him. My step-father was the man that I was supposed to respect and look up to as if he was the father I never had. "*The man of the house*" He was supposed to protect, love and look after me. The title just wouldn't sit properly with me; I never could call him "*dad*".

"This man isn't my father, and he could never be a father to me. He was the worst role model to have as a father!

I began to withdraw. The facade soon fell away, the big expectations of what a father should be were shattered, and I gave up on my dreams of ever wanting a father. Eventually, I had grown up and grown fed up with his inappropriateness, behaviour and disrespect.

I soon vented my anger and bitterness by standing up to him in his face and shout in defence for my mother. There was a day we had argued for well over an hour as my mum stood on the side-lines. I was tired, hot and frustrated. I just wanted to get out of the house. Our arguing was a frequent occurrence, it was agreed a lock could be put on my door to keep him away when I needed space. A lock on a door wasn't enough for the mental torture I endured. The arguments would continue, getting louder and more heated. My mum would deal with his drunken outbursts and accept it. She never argued back. It wasn't in her nature. I don't know how she felt or why she couldn't stick up for herself. I knew it wasn't right. If my mother couldn't defend herself, how was she to protect me? All those years of depression and sadness for my mother came creeping back. Her life seemed to revolve around the attention and acceptance of a man. I'd continue arguing with him every few days, and as my frustrations grew, so did my outlet. I began smashing things in my room. As I stop in a moment of anger, I slide down the wall and cry with my face in my arms. I look up through my watery eyes and see my room; my belongings on the floor, shelves off the wall. Upset, I saw my beloved dolphin snow globe, something sentimental that had been with me throughout my childhood. I was so angry. So much of me was slowly being destroyed by this man. My innocence, my home, my room. As my door was locked, I let out a scream and threw the globe and smashed it against the wall. Sobbing, sitting on the floor because it was my favourite item from my childhood. I sat there, and I meditated over the fragments of glass for a while. The thought to cut my arms came in and this was the first time I started self-harming. I made a vow to myself that I would never allow a man ever to have the same hold on me!

- 17 - | B R A V E

My mum sent me to spend more time with my older cousins to control my rebellious behaviour. Spending time with older cousins led me to experimenting with smoking cigarettes and marijuana.

September 2004

My mum was expecting a baby. United, they would have their child now, and this baby would have a real biological father and a real family. Something I never had. After all, I wasn't the perfect daughter he had anticipated. Their news pushed me to withdraw more and more, which worsened my confidence. Meanwhile, I had transitioned into my second year of High School in Year 8. But I felt more grown up from spending so much time with my older cousin's. I had matured and was admired for carrying myself so well and acting a lot older than my age. As I began to spend time with my aunty, I could see that my mother wasn't like the others and I began to resent her. I hated that she was weak and allowed a man to take control of her life. I hated that I had not received any love. I hated that my biological father was somewhere, free and living his life, while I was living in such hell and daily torment. I didn't allow myself to love her or her partner. I would not let myself have any form of emotional attachment to them. I was very embarrassed by my mother and her partner. I would detach myself, go out with friends and gain more freedom.

I knew my mother always chose her boyfriend over me. Regularly, they would leave on the weekends, thinking it was good to give me my space, so they could pursue their relationship. She would ensure I would not tell anyone. I appreciated having the house to myself though, as any teenager would. It mainly was enjoyable as it meant that I wouldn't be arguing with my step-dad. Initially, I loved acting grown up, as though I lived on my own. Watching what I wanted, smoking, getting high, drinking as I pleased and going to sleep late. However, this slowly advanced my feelings of rejection and abandonment. It soon became even more isolating and cold. I then began to throw myself more into my friendships and try to be popular at school. I made friends with the 'wrong crowd'; with those that were older and who like me, enjoyed smoking.

Popularity soon became my worst enemy. It was great at first, everyone knowing your name and having respect towards you. Until it all came tumbling down at school and amounted to nothing. I soon lost all my friends because I hardly attended school. They didn't like me mixing with the wrong crowds. I had begun to meddle with drugs and alcohol, and I was a changed person. No one knew the battles I faced at home. My school was my escape until it too became a place I hated, so I then began truanting from school.

January 2005

In January 2005, my next-door neighbour Maria had lost her battle to cancer and died a prolonged and painful death. I had never known death before. Her death was hard for me to come to terms with. To add to this, I was to discover news that would eventually push me over the edge. News which would push me to my breaking point.

My step-father's niece had accused him of attempted rape! His flat was raided by police and forensics had taken various items away for further investigation. He was arrested and taken into custody for questioning.

That was the second blow, like when you're waiting for a bus, and two come at once. Hit with a second bus, I didn't know whether to run or cry. My step-father's niece being only a few years older than me, made me become so frightened and feel at such unease. I was in an utter state of shock, *"That could have been me?"*

The news sent me into a darker place, feeling unsafe within my own home, dealing with emotional withdrawal and rejection from my mother. I turned deeper into drugs to help me feel comforted and numb the pain of my emotions.

I had no one to talk to at all. After all, this isn't something you can go running to school and tell your friends. If I did say something to someone, rumours could spread that my step-dad was a paedophile. With no one to confide in, a rush of inward battles ran through my mind. I had no place to express my emotions, so I could only suppress them through tears and drug abuse.

Through it all, my mother chose to stay with him - Even if he had attempted to rape his niece. Two months later, my 13th birthday, came and went. Being a teenager, I did not care of this new season of life. I felt tarnished, traumatised and numb to life. Since self-harming with the broken snow globe, it had progressed into smoking drugs and now the newly learnt abuse of prescribed medication. In my fit of rage, anger and upset, I usually would load myself with prescribed tablets to calm myself. (The medication I took was prescribed to my mother to manage her depression and epilepsy). This soon started becoming the norm and my way of dealing with situations. In this time, I was also suffering from bulimia, purely out of self-hate. My doctor referred me for counselling, and it was with my counsellor that I disclosed my self-harming. She was concerned and told my mum, and the counsellor advised for all medication to immediately be hidden and locked away. My mum being ignorant to the severity of the counsellor's plea, put the medication in a bag under her bed, which remained easily accessible. Prescription abuse, however, would quickly become the death of me.

CHAPTER
3

Enough is Enough

Suicide

Most kids look forward to becoming a teenager. I, on the other hand, already faced the realities of life, and I couldn't stand the real world.

Already I had witnessed too much for my tender years. Having a sex offender too close for comfort was killing me on the inside. He'd make my skin crawl. You could see in his drunken gaze that he was eyeing me up and down, a sense that would make any female feel uncomfortable.

I no longer wanted to feel a part of my family.

Resentment towards my mother grew even more for choosing her partner over me, and I did not have or show any love towards her. She was by this point heavily pregnant, and I regularly would go out with friends. Anything to avoid being at home. I wasn't looking after her or helping around the house. Although I was rebellious, and my mum would put it down to 'teenage' behaviour, there was more to it. Deep down, I was crying out for help, looking for love, acceptance, and safety. No one knew the inward battles I was facing.

One month after I had turned 13, I had decided that *enough was enough*. During this time, I began seriously contemplating life and found myself in a dark, depressive and desperate place. Thoughts such as "*if I wasn't around anymore (death), the world would still go on, and that no one would even care if I wasn't alive"*. I believed that *"my life had no meaning"*. It was then I began to imagine what life would look like if I were no longer around. I realised that life would still go on and my departure would not affect anyone. I began planning to commit suicide.

April 2005

In April 2005 shortly after turning 13, I would carry out the most dangerous act that could claim my life. The days leading up to April 13th were dark and dreary. I was high on drugs for the two weeks leading up, drinking alcohol and wandering the streets with friends like a zombie. My mum and step-dad knew I was always high and would only shout and tell me off. One week before that devastating day, I remember coming off a bus, high as a kite and a woman stopped my friends and me. She began saying that *"Jesus is coming back; the world is going to end soon. You'll hear of wars, rumours of wars, cataclysmic weather"*. We didn't take much notice, but her words made sense to me even in that moment of intoxication.

Wednesday 13th April 2005

It was a warm evening around p.m. and spring had fully emerged. By this stage I had stopped going to school. I had returned home from a day out of hanging with gangs on the streets, only to eat some food. My mother tried to talk to me about my new way of life, with drugs and wrong friends. I was so annoyed by her efforts of care. It angered me. I argued that her choice of a wrong boyfriend was worse than mine!

Having already made up my mind; it was too late. My mother's sudden cause for concern hurt me.

I stormed out of the room after our heated discussion and went to my bedroom, locking the door behind me. I went in and blared my music to drown the sound of my screams. I processed my anger and hate towards my mother, step-father, life, my biological father and the world who never loved me.

I look to my right and see the remnants of tablets from previous times of taking pills. Although the packets were empty, I wanted more!

Out of such despair, I crept around the house in search of a lot more boxes of medication. I remembered the boxes under my mum's bed. I collected such an amount, more than I had ever consumed before. I returned to my room and locked the door. I built up my anger again and watched myself in the mirror. With tears gushing down my face, I hated what I saw. Knowing this was it, no one was even here to try to stop me.

I opened the boxes of medication and created a pile of them, and I grabbed the handful of tablets and began stuffing my mouth and using a cup of water to wash them down. The last pills were lying on the stand, staring at me. As I look at them, the taste of the coating on the tablets was so disgusting, they were all stuck in my throat. I couldn't possibly take any more.

I could barely take any more without the feeling of needing to gag. I had now overdosed on a mixture of anti-depressants, painkillers and epileptic medication. As the taste of them made their way down my throat, I unlocked my door and walked outside to smoke a cigarette to diminish the flavour.

My mother then walked up to me, after having had a look in my room, to see what I had been doing in that time. And she stands there with the remnants of the empty blister packs I had just digested in her hands. Crossly she demands to know, *"what have you done?"*

Immediately, I storm out from the garden and out the side of the house, frustrated by her sudden cause for concern, again!

"It's too late!", I cry from within.

As I leave the house to avoid confrontation, I struggle. I barely made it a few steps.

Staggering, in that same spot, the place that carried solemn memories. It was the exact place I had fallen off my bike all those years ago. That place where my dad should have been teaching me to ride my bike. Again, in such a crucial moment of my life, my dad should have been there for me. The ground beneath me was moving on its axis, I was dizzy, and began to blackout. Everything was moving at a much slower speed, and I could hear weird noises.

I felt extremely intoxicated. The medication from my overdose had begun to take effect.

Only managing a few steps away from outside the house, my mother appears from behind. She takes me by the arm and ushers me back into the house – not wanting to cause a scene.

If she hadn't come to find me, I would have collapsed there and then on the road. I was so profoundly drugged up and sedated. My body followed, but I was slowly losing my consciousness.

Staggering into the house, as if I had just returned from a drunken night out, I slumped on the sofa. I recall drowsily murmuring, "*I just want to go to sleep, I just want to go to sleep*", my mum rushes to the kitchen to get me water…
As I mumble those words, now at a much slower pace:
"*I just want - to - go - to*",

my eyes slowly begin to close, my peripheral vision reduces dramatically,

I manage to softly murmur the word "*Sleep*". Every blink gets heavier and my eyesight becomes smaller, until they shut…

That was the last I recall of Wednesday April 13th, 2005

CHAPTER

4

She's Just Sleeping

The following account has been compiled from
eyewitnesses, health professionals and police records used
during the investigations leading up to my near-death
experience.

What continued that evening, was my mother bringing me
back in the house. As I slumped on the sofa, my mother
went to get me water. By the time she had come back she
thought I had fallen asleep. However, I had not fallen
asleep. I had lost consciousness. Throughout the night my mum had
sent her partner to check on me to ensure I was ok. I was gurgling
noises as I struggled to breathe but he thought I was still ok; if I was
breathing. Both unaware of the seriousness of the circumstances.

Thursday 14th April 2005

7/7:30 a.m. the following morning; my mum and partner try to wake
me for school.

I lay there lifeless, gurgling noises as I struggle to breathe because of
the foam that had accumulated in my mouth. My eyes rolled
backwards, not closed properly. My mother and her partner had tried
to wake me up. But there was no response. The months leading up to
my overdose, I had been severely truanting from school, my school
head of year Mr Dean had called that same morning to demand that

I come to school or further action would be taken My attendance was less than twice a week. If I did attend, I'd go to school late in the day, or go in and leave after a few hours.

As Mr Dean was making these threats, my mother told him she was doing her best to get me to come to school, but she could not wake me up. He then questioned why I wasn't waking up. My mums partner then takes the phone, *"she's just sleeping"*, *"She won't wake up"*, *"she's been taking lots of tablets over the last couple of days"*, *"she has been overdosing"*.

Directly, Mr Dean told him *"put the phone down and call for an ambulance!"*

Not grasping the severity of the situation, my mum then called what at the time was NHS Direct, this is a number you call for advice and information if the matter is not life-threatening. Once communicated with the operator, they had instantly notified the emergency services and arranged for an ambulance to be dispatched. Within minutes, sirens were heard from a distance, the sound getting closer and louder. The reflection of flashing blue lights was seen through the windows.

8 a.m. an ambulance and four police cars had arrived at my address. The house cordoned off, police tape sealed around the house.

'POLICE LINE DO NOT CROSS'

The commotion caused a stir. My neighbours, some still in their dressing gowns gathered outside, questioning what this early morning disturbance was. Paramedics attend to my lifeless body, with one opening my eyes and flashing a light, *"Hello Tanya, can you hear me"*; and the other opening a bag to retrieve equipment. The paramedics look at one another *"She's non-responsive"*. They tell my mum with urgency *"she needs serious medical attention from the hospital"* My step-dad tells the paramedics he wants to stay with me. Meanwhile, the police are outside closing off the road.

Paramedics wheel me on a stretcher into the back of the ambulance. Slamming the doors shut, they leave the scene and rush to the nearest hospital.

Sirens are wailing, blue lights flashing, racing through London's rush-hour traffic. The paramedics were trying everything they could to bring me to consciousness. While in the ambulance, the drugs in my system created a severe reaction resulting in a toxic seizure; due to the depressed levels of my consciousness. My step-dad begins crying, pleading with me to be strong and pull through, as he holds my hand. Convulsing, the paramedics tried in vain to control the seizure and the ambulance had to be halted on a busy road as they attempted to save my life. My entire body convulsing, lifting off the trolley and thudding back down. This moment in time, is make or break.

My life is dramatically slipping away and after a minute of convulsing, I go limp. The ambulance is less than 60 seconds' drive from the hospital. Upon entering A&E, immediately doctors and nurses fought to save my life. *"This is Tanya Sandhu, a 13-year-old female; she had taken an overdose of amitriptyline and phenytoin with painkillers yesterday around 1800' hours, Amitriptyline is a very toxic overdose"*.

There and then, the Doctors and Nurses go into action. My step-dad is held back and asked to wait at the door. He watches through the glass window. Small sticky electrodes were attached to my chest. The defibrillators charged, they shout *"CLEAR"* as a shock is used to bring me back to consciousness. My body jumps into the air from the shock. A moment of silence. No response. Nothing. They monitor my heartbeat. My heart beating slow, the pace medically recognised as life threatening. Oxygen continually pumped into my stomach. An intubation tube was inserted up my nose and down my throat to aide my breathing. They administer an infusion to try to remove the toxicity of the overdose from my body. This was done at a high concentration, in the bid to regulate my heart rate.

At this moment in time, the specialists had liaised with the critical response team from other hospitals. They were advised that I be transferred to a specialist hospital; I needed specialist help.

It had now been 12 hours since I had taken my overdose.
With the intubation tubes and wires in place, I'm escorted to the roof of the building. Doctors wheel me to a waiting helicopter, the machines are attached to the bed. Without delay I'm airlifted to St Mary's hospital in Paddington's, Central London's Intensive Care Unit.
As soon as I approach the doors to the Intensive Care Unit, the doctors who are desperately awaiting my arrival, are made aware of my status.

After hours of around-the-clock care, I am on a life support machine and intubation to help me breathe, to keep me alive. I was in a **stable but extremely critical state.** I was now in a coma on a life support machine following a Toxic, Life-Threatening Overdose. My future unknown. The doctors and nurses could only monitor, waiting to observe what the outcome could be. The possibilities of my survival are now very frail and lying in the fate of the machines. I lay there, lifeless, an intubation tube down my throat and tubes up my nose. I had wires across my chest and drips attached to my hands. The life support machine to my left was pumping up and down to help me breathe. A noise and sight unimaginable, and one you'd never wish to see a loved one in.

News had spread to family and friends and in my school of what had happened. Family arranged flights from out of England to be at my bedside. Frantically, cousins and family began arriving at the hospital. My mum arrives, heavily pregnant. Not wanting to go into early labour, everyone tries to keep her calm. As my family were still unaware of exactly what had happened, they call on my step-dad to inform them of the intense previous 24-hours.

Intensive Care Treatment

It was now two days of worry, fear, tears and sleeplessness.
In the waiting area, my family huddled together, drinking hot drinks of coffee to keep them awake and alert. They hoped that there would be some positive news. Then, a nurse approached, and she gently guided them into a family liaison room.
As they walk into the room, behind the door is the Doctor and Specialists. My family were then prepared for the worst thing that they had anticipated. My death!
I could die. The build-up of the previous days had prepared them for this very moment. They had been made aware of the realities of my future but did not expect it to come to pass. The medical professionals had little confidence I would survive.

They explained *"It would soon be drawing in three days, of which Tanya hasn't made any improvement"*. The time was drawing near to switch off the machines. If they were to turn the machines off, I would die! No more second chances, no last goodbye, no hugs to say I love you. No rescue from my biological father on his horse, to relieve me of my pain. The acts of my overdose would have been goodbye. The Doctor explained *"If, and there was a small 'if', Tanya did pull through from the coma and survive this ordeal, due to the severity of what transpired, the time between her overdose and receiving the right medical help, she could end up having brain damage or severe kidney/liver degeneration. The outcome is unknown. The Tanya you once knew, may never come back. She would need around the clock help, and your lives could change forever"*. He then concluded: *"We will be looking at turning the machines off, tomorrow"*. During those moments there was a physical and spiritual battle for my life.

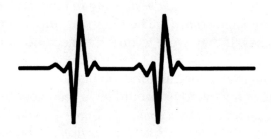

CHAPTER

5

Bright Lights

Three days after I had taken my overdose, I slowly start gaining consciousness, barely making out the *bright lights* in the ceiling from above me.

The morning after the doctors had told my family that the time was soon approaching to turn the machines off. I started to make an independent response and my heart began beating at a steady rate. I started breathing on my own. I had survived my overdose and woken up from the coma!

It was a miracle! I was no longer in a coma. I had pulled through from this catastrophic event and was now alive.

Stirring, slowly opening my eyes, I was just able to make out the hospital lighting on the ceiling over me. The sound of my own heartbeat on a hospital machine. Barely conscious, coming in and out of consciousness. A nurse inclines over me to adjust the monitor next to me. Stroking my hair and smiling, she tells me I'm ok, *"You took an overdose"* she says, *"but you are going to be ok"*. Slowly, she begins to pull the tubes from the life support machine out of my nose and from out of my throat. The tubes being removed from my nose and throat was a sensation that was so intensely painful, I have never experienced anything so excruciating! The side effects of the drugs from my overdose were still active. I was heavily medicated, I could only lay there, unable to react.

"What day was it? How long have I been here?", these questions would slowly come and go in my mind.

She brushed my teeth, and slowly fed me liquid foods and water through a straw.

The very doctors and nurses that would continue to assess me were the same staff that had aided in saving my life. It made me feel like they cared. I wondered what made them feel that my life was worth saving. Then I heard those same depressive, suicidal voices. I reasoned that it was because of their job that they saved me not because they cared about me. Over the next few days, I would steadily regain normalities, and begin to talk and walk. I had been declared stable, and no longer in need for specialist care. I was then transferred to a general ward, where I would recover under careful mental health watch from professionals for two weeks. I was under assessment by mental health professionals, therapists, and psychologists.

CHAPTER

6

Foster Care

When I had woken from the coma, I didn't know what had happened properly. Now out of the Intensive Care Unit and recovering on a ward, I was surrounded by flowers, balloons and get-well-soon cards. Some of my family members were in the room who I hadn't seen for years. Yet they had travelled from different parts of the country to visit. Everyone was extra friendly to me, but there was a massive elephant in the room; I had tried to kill myself!

No one dared ask me questions. I was spoken about rather than spoken to. They were treading on eggshells around me, not wanting to upset me, not wanting anything to provoke me to overdose again. It made me feel as though I had a sign on my bedpost,

'WARNING – APPROACH WITH CAUTION'

My 2-week admission in the hospital was challenging, and I became so bored of the same surroundings. Fast forward a few days, and no one came to visit me anymore. The flowers were wilting, the balloons deflated. I seemed to have been forgotten.

A girl was admitted in the same ward and put next to my bed. She too had attempted suicide, hers not as severe. Her entire family would visit every day without fail, bringing her home comforts; ice cream, food, her personal belongings. She was kind enough to bring me in and allow me to have some company and share her food.

However, she soon was discharged within a few days, leaving me on my own again.

After two weeks it was confirmed that there was nothing wrong with my physical health. I defeated the odds of what the doctors had said would happen to me. No brain damage, no kidney or liver failure. I survived that ordeal with not one thing wrong with my health!

I was not allowed to return to my family home. Although nothing was physically wrong with me, the life-threatening overdose I had committed meant that I had to be assessed further within a Mental Health Unit.

Towards the end of my admission in hospital, a nurse walks over and tells me I have a phone call. "*A call?*", I thought. *Who could be calling me?* Intrigued, barefoot I tip-toe to the reception desk. Picking up the handset I draw it under my short brown hair to my ear, and this mystery person introduces himself as *"John Churchill"*, "*I'm a social worker for Ealing Social Services*" he asked: "*do you know what happened to you?*" Trying to understand the reason for his call, I cleared my throat and responded quietly, "*I tried to kill myself.*" He continues, "*your mother neglected you, and because you were not given immediate medical attention you nearly died. That is neglect, did you know that?*".

John went on to say, "*We want to admit you to a mental health hospital for five days of the week to make sure you will be ok, and you will be placed with a family in short-term foster care the other two, so you can stay close by to the hospital*". I'm then asked to pass the phone to the receptionist, and in return, she passes me a form with a pen.

It asks me about my personal information, address, ethnicity, and religion. My ethnicity has always been an uncommonness. Half Polish and half Indian, I never met anyone growing up that I could identify with ethnically. My ethnicity gave me many identity issues, especially my religion. Although I was not a practising Christian, I always believed there was a God and I grew up observing Easter as the time when Jesus died on the cross. I stated my faith as Christian.

A few days later, the nurse tells me to pack my belongings. Today would be the day I get to go home. I did wonder why no family had come to visit to take me home? Feelings of my childhood flood back to the times my mum couldn't collect me because she didn't drive, this wasn't uncommon.

A man then walks down the corridor in a suit holding a briefcase. John Churchill introduces himself as the man on the phone. He explained that my mother was told to stay at home, and he would be driving me there to collect a few clothes. I am discharged from hospital and directed to his car. It was now over two weeks since I had attempted to commit suicide. I remember the day I left the hospital, it was a grey, dark and dismal Thursday. As we reach my house, I see my heavily pregnant mother and her partner waiting at the window. John tells me to be quick and gather a few of my belongings. I get out of the car, and I ring the doorbell. I'm welcomed by my mother and her partner, although my mum does not seem aware that this could mean I may never live with her again.

I walk into my bedroom. The last memory I have of this room was the scene of where I carried out the life-threatening overdose that nearly claimed my life. It was the left overs of a crime scene, I notice many of my belongings had been removed as police evidence. I sit for a moment to take it all in. Then I slowly begin to pack a few belongings.

As I walk back to the front room, John is sitting with my mum, and he gets her to sign a green piece of paper. One for her to keep and one for me. From that point, I became a registered child to Social Services.

I was amazed as to how quickly, without hesitation she signed me away. No tears, no questioning, no hesitation, no fighting. Given away, over and done. She knew she had made a serious mistake not calling for medical help sooner. The severity of my near-death experience had shaken her up so much, she couldn't question, couldn't argue. She was scared, heavily pregnant and obliged with whatever Social Services said.

There I am 13-year-old Tanya, with what is materialistically my life made, to fit into a cabin sized suitcase. I am only supposed to be away for six weeks to this mental health hospital.

I, therefore, pack what any teenager would pack; a whole bunch of CDs', personal items and a 'few' clothes. What I did not know, is that I wouldn't be moving back in 6 weeks' time. I said my goodbyes and shared quick hugs. My mum stayed in the house, and my step-dad walked me to the car. He had been with me every step of the way during my hospital admission. He had softened towards me and was sad to see me go. John drives off. I sit in the passenger's seat watching my reflection in the window and quietly observe all I see on the way. I had just nearly died, and the world looked different to me. The dark overcast gloom made my clouded view seem even more real to me. The fact that I could have been dead, and my thoughts were correct – The world would still go on.

My mind wandered back to my mum. She had just signed me away. I thought she would have cried, and I could have cried too, if she only held me or told me how she felt.

The busyness of my thoughts didn't allow me to process appropriately how quickly my mum gave me away. My focus changed to anticipate what could be ahead of me. *Who will these Foster carers be?* My understanding of Foster Carers formed from what I had heard in the media of money hungry, negligent, abuse scandals. Somehow, this didn't scare me. I was appreciative that if they were neglectful pushovers, then at least I would be able to continue with my drug taking, smoking, drinking and nights out.

We arrive at a house, John speaks with an Ethiopian woman, she closes the door. He comes back all flustered, and his cheeks flushed red from embarrassment, with paperwork falling out of his hands. This house turned out to be my Foster Carers old address! Trying to hold his briefcase, balancing the paperwork without the wind blowing it away and holding a phone to his ear, he walks back to the car. He stands outside of the car with his briefcase on the roof, talking on his mobile phone trying to find out the new address. Not too long after, he's notified of the update. He then rummages through his boot for a map. He sits in the driver's seat, locates the address and we disembark for the final time.

The car pulls up to the correct house, I peer from the passenger's seat to get a glimpse of who these carers could be. John leaves me in the car to make sure this is the right house. As he walks back more calmly, I knew it was the right house. I get out and collect my suitcase from the backseat and walk towards the house. It had ivy covering its pebbled walls, with the front door on the side of the house.

As I walk up the drive a Mediterranean looking woman comes out the door, and I am taken aback by her glow, this wasn't just beauty. I could see something more radiant about her. Something from the inside shone through. She welcomes me with a warm smile and hugs me. Her hug immediately makes me feel welcomed. As I enter in the hallway, I am led to the stairs straight to the bedroom where I would be staying. As we walk up to my bedroom, I sit in this neatly made room and spot a wardrobe.

I daydream losing the conversation, quietly thinking to myself the fun of being able to place my clothes in there. I had never had a cupboard for my clothes, and this would be the first! My Social worker talks about the six-week rehabilitation programme in a Mental Health Hospital, with the long-term plan being for me to eventually return me to my family home.

A few weeks passed, and I settled into my new life.

The day approaches where I was due for an induction at Edgware Hospital's Mental Health Unit. The night before, my carer sits me down and asks me intently, "*Tanya, I don't think you're crazy. I know you're not crazy. But you go there (to the hospital), have a look and see whether you feel this would be suitable for you. If you don't want to go – you don't have to*".

Her affirmation gave me a sense of confidence and a never experienced reassurance. Someone believed in me. My mother had never fought for me; she freely gave custody of me to Social Services. On the other hand, here was someone who didn't even know me, and was willing to support my choice. I had family members who were talking about me, saying that I must have mental health problems to try to commit suicide. Then here I was, sitting with a woman, a stranger who barely knew me, who was not related to me, and she was showing so much love and speaking such life over me.

CHAPTER
7

Mental Hospital

T
he following day I went to Edgware Hospital knowing I had a choice. As I arrive at the mental health unit, I notice a teenager around 16 years old walking out of the foyer to smoke a cigarette. She looked disorientated and had a dark aura about her. I was happy to see we'd freely be allowed to smoke. I am then met by one of the staff members who guides me around the facility.

There are approximately 6-8 other teens who I would be joining. He shows me their rooms, then adds that I'd often be evacuated in the middle of the night as the young people frequently set the fire alarms off. After the tour, I am then left to spend half an hour with the young people. They were very happy to see a new face. We talk about day-to-day life in the ward, some having been there for years. This same girl I had just seen in the foyer walks in, and she is the only one to not greet me, she just doesn't say a word. She doesn't seem to say a word to anyone.

She walks straight passed me to a corner as if she didn't see me and began to sit there rocking. I knew that something wasn't right with her.

The teens then start to ask me about what happened to make me come here. I tell them I attempted to commit suicide, and they ask me eagerly, *"what method did you use?"*, I tell them "*an overdose*". They then all lean closer around me, and one guy, rolls up his sleeve to show deep scars of physical self-harm. I remember distinctively one girl raising her chin to show me various scars on her neck from where she had unsuccessfully tried to hang herself. She told me *"It didn't work the first time, so I tried **again**!"* I spent a while with them. It was interesting, seeing their new-found way of life. I thought because they didn't go to school, they were free, but they weren't. Quite overwhelmed by it all, I began thinking if I really wanted to stay here? They were all lovely but from speaking with them, I could tell they genuinely did have deep rooted issues. Their calmness was created by their medication.

I knew I wasn't as mentally troubled as they were. Heavily medicated, I could see that a lot of them did have mental health issues. I knew that I wasn't unwell, mentally, my overdose was me crying out for the pain to end. My mind then wanders to my new-found foster home. I was happy staying with my foster carers for a while, and I decided not to attend the rehabilitation programme.

I left the ward and when I was collected by my foster parents, they asked me how it was. I was open and told them my experience and that I didn't want to go back. They did not question it. They supported my decision!

Saturday 21st May 2005

That evening, after I had visited the mental health hospital, I would have a conversation that would help my life make sense.

I was in my room when I was called downstairs to talk with my foster carer. We sat in the front room of the house on the sofa, and it was a beautiful warm evening. The conversation then led to the topic of my overdose, and my carer asked:

"What made you attempt to take your own life, Tanya?" In the silence of my lack of response, she then spoke to me in a way I had never heard before. She told me quite firmly but so lovingly:

"Tanya, did you know your life is significant and that your life is not your own to take…God gave you this life, and He has a plan for you!" She went on to tell me that, *"God knew you before you were in your mother's womb.*

He had planned you from the very beginning...and has a great plan and purpose for your life. You didn't come to us or this house by mistake. God saved your life. You could have died."

I sat there quietly taking it in, trying to make sense of it all. I had never heard anything like this in my life; but somehow, I knew what she was saying to be true, it made sense. *"The devil wanted to kill you because God has a plan for your life and God wants to use you. He has given you a story, a story that you will go to share with people across the world."* As she mentioned about me sharing my story, a picture appeared in my mind – I see me sharing my story with thousands of people in a stadium!

Her following words resonated in me: *"God is the Father you have never had, and He's better than your earthly father ever could be. There is a space in your heart that only God can fulfil. He is the dad you've been longing for."*

I had always yearned for a father – she did not know this!

There was always a hole in my heart, a hole that was yearning for my daddy. To know that I had a Father, a Heavenly Father was so reassuring. Mainly, to hear that He is one that will be and can always be with me. My mind instantly took me back to my childhood, the days when I cried myself to sleep talking to God.

Maybe *He was real? Perhaps He had listened to me? Was this His way of answering me?*

She then resumed the conversation telling me, she and her husband owned a church and that I was more than welcome to come. I never actually knew what they did, so this answered that question, as I was continuing to unveil who this family was. I remember the first time I had seen her husband. The entire family, arriving with three cars between them, met in a car park to enter the restaurant together. As he got out of his car, there was a glow and positive aura around him. I saw a white light as if the sun was shining from behind him, yet it was a dark gloomy, grey day.

Here I was a suicidal 13-year-old girl, placed into the care of a Pastor and his wife, God had used wrong for good and used this as an opportunity to meet with me, where I was. This orchestration of events would change my life, for the course of eternity.

Months passed, and I began visiting the church, seeing people dancing, clapping, singing to God. It reminded me of school. We used to sing songs to God, songs such as; He's got the whole world in His hands, Hosanna, Shalom, and morning prayers in assembly. I was witnessing people becoming Christians by allowing Jesus to become the Lord of their life.

Intrigued by it all I believed Jesus was real.

During the Summer of 2005 at 13 years old, I too eventually, asked Jesus to come into my life.

CHAPTER

8

If You're Real?

I remember a travelling Evangelist had visited my church. He was touring the UK, sharing his compelling life story, and I now discovered it wasn't just happening to me. God was changing lives all over the world!

Not only had God given me such a unique story, there were many others! As the evangelist shared his story, he spoke of how God had been with him every step of the way until a point came in his life when Jesus was knocking on the door of his heart. I had always known of Jesus, that He was a historical figure, a man on a cross. Someone whose name was used continuously in vain. But now here I was discovering that He, Jesus was much more than a historical figure. He was real! Jesus had come into this world, for the salvation of humanity.

Jesus endured a gruesome and harrowing death, beaten, rejected, shamefully hung and nailed to a tree! That was for me! When Jesus was on the cross every drop of blood was shed for my forgiveness. My life now began to make sense.

As this man finished sharing his story, he then gave the opportunity for anyone to let Jesus into their heart. He questioned the audience asking if we knew where we were going when we died?

Death had always been something I questioned. I did not know what happens after death. Now I was provided a reassurance of eternal life, in Heaven. By this point, I already felt like I was Christian, but I hadn't asked Jesus to come and live inside of me. There was a moment when the speaker requested people to close their eyes, to give an opportunity for anyone to stand and say "*yes*", to open their heart to Jesus. I remember sitting there and discreetly looking around as people would rise to accept Jesus, and as they did the audience began to clap.

Before, I knew it I could see a person stand from the corner of my eye, another round of applause. Then I hear another round of applause - this time, the applaud was for me; I was standing!

How did I, I don't even remember standing up, but before I knew it, there I was standing, and I just whispered in the loudness of the clapping and rejoicing "*Jesus, if you're real, reveal yourself to me*".

I stood up at that altar call and surrendered my life to Jesus. Nothing super spiritual happened to me, and I didn't feel anything change on the outside, but on the inside, for once, I was feeling good! I felt lighter, confident and free.

I believed I had something to look forward to, a fresh start, a new beginning. I had just become a born-again Christian!

Throughout my life, I had yearned for my biological father. There had always been a hole in my heart, a longing. I had been looking for love in all the wrong places. I tried to fill my void with smoking, drugs, even an attempted suicide!

Now I knew that the hole in my heart was a void only *Jesus* could fill.

My death would not have been the end of my pain. That would have just been the beginning. Suicide is a permanent solution to a temporary problem. I still would have had the void of eternal separation from my creator and damnation in hell. Only Jesus was the solution to that hole in my heart. By Him restoring me to my Heavenly Father.

As I had mentioned in the Chapter before when I filled in my forms for Social Services, the fact that I had written Christian and a mixed

Asian/European ethnicity on my form is what led to me placed with this specific family. There are no accidents with God, no coincidences. Everything is carefully thought out, mastered, orchestrated and planned by God and is a part of His much more significant story! You are the ethnicity you are, live where you live and born the day you were born for a part of the bigger picture – Gods bigger picture.

That form is what was used to place me with this specific family. Over time I started getting more involved with my new-found church community, being welcomed by the congregation and embraced with open arms.

When I gave my life to Jesus, I had a new-found confidence. I had a reason to live. Knowing the meaning of life, I was no longer afraid of death. My life became brighter.

Although I had been separated from what I knew of my earthly family I felt adopted into a new family. A family of God. The church I joined was had a strong 400 + congregation, so it was hard not to feel their embrace. That Summer of 2005 was so fun. I joined the youth group and we regularly spent time together, went on day trips and hosted youth events. Never had I productively spent time with young people before. All I was accustomed to was smoking, hanging out on the streets and getting high. Now I had purpose and a sense of belonging.

Everyone at the church was so loving and accepting of me. They looked out for me as one of their own. Life, hope, and destiny frequently declared over me, and I would begin to feel confident enough to share my story of how I had attempted to commit suicide.

I remember my Foster Mum asking me on a Saturday night if I wanted to tell the church, the following morning my testimony. *"What is my testimony?"* I asked her. She sat me down and explained that every Christian has a testimony. *"It is your story of how you came to know Jesus"*. Together we wrote a few points down. I was so nervous! I hardly slept that night, wondering how I would speak. *What if I opened my mouth and nothing came out?*

The next morning in church, sitting in the second row. I am introduced by the Pastor and his wife as their Foster Daughter and as I move my head glued watching my feet as I walk up the pulpit. I was too nervous to look up at the four hundred plus people. I was handed the microphone and look out into the audience and open my mouth. I begin sharing about my childhood.

When I get to the part of how I found Jesus (even though He found me) it was like *'whoosh'* a surge of electricity or energy. I was shouting passionately, like a jumping jack I began getting excited talking about Jesus and the members of the church stand and begin to clap and cheer me on in agreement. I no longer was nervous and felt so happy to share my story. As I finish there is a standing ovation of clappers, cheerers and people that were so happy. As I make my way back to my seat, they hug me, congratulate me, shake my hand. They were amazed at my story. Being only thirteen and sharing so confidently. It was Jesus, I felt in that moment, that being a Christian was who I really was.

I was born to speak about Jesus!

Gradually, speaking publicly about my overdose, helped me overcome the feelings of embarrassment and shame associated with that part of my life. It started increasing my confidence. It was a story which helped me show people how real Jesus was to me. As I attended church more I learnt on forgiveness. How to forgive my mum, step-dad, my biological dad and everyone who had ever hurt me; to be able to love them just as Jesus had loved me.

Although, social services didn't allow for me to return to my mum's care. I did my best to take it in my stride. It was hard at times but those were the circumstances. That aside, life was going so well for me. The thoughts of suicide never re-entered my mind.

September 2005

Five months after I attempted to commit suicide. My foster mother said that she thought it was only right for me to return to main stream school and complete education. It had been nearly an entire academic year since I had been truanting from school. I enrolled at a new school in North-West London, Kingsbury High.

I settled into life in mainstream school, and I would visit a psychotherapist once a week for one year. As I grew in my faith in Jesus, I felt that I no longer benefited from attending my appointments.

It got to the stage when I remember my psycho-therapist Abi, asking me *"Tanya when you're feeling alone and need someone to talk to, who do you talk to?* "I confidently responded *"God!"*. She looked up over her nose toward me, stopped writing her notes, and she questioned rudely: *"But what about a person Tanya, a real person"*. To which, I repeated smiling, *"Yes, God – He's real!"* I gained a sense of peace that helped me, something that was not gained through my counselling sessions. Counselling was therapeutic, it was an outlet to discuss what issues I was facing to a certain degree. However, she didn't understand my new-found faith. I felt she could only relate to me on a surface level. She couldn't help my soul. The only real help I found in life was knowing there was a God. My life was gradually changing for the better. My personality had transformed. I no longer was the timid, shy Tanya.

I would pray for friends and family. I would share Jesus with my old friends who still smoked, took drugs and lived carelessly at the weekends. Yet the more I began to spend time with Jesus and start a relationship with Him, the desire to be around such negativity didn't sit right with me. I'd pray for them, but I slowly drifted into new friendship circles and began embarking on new focuses and looked forward to seeing my church community.

Having been thrown into church, given my Foster Carer's were the Senior Pastors was a blessing, as I would not have had the confidence to attend a church had I not been taken by my carers. However, there were deep-rooted relational insecurities that were lurking and had not been dealt with. As much as I loved God and He loved me, I didn't fully understand my new identity as a Christian. I was a young teenager and still yearned for relationships to fulfil my loneliness. I had given my life to Christ but there were so many distractions, demons and disappointments for me to stay on the straight and narrow. During the weekends I would go out and stay out as much as possible. Although I would always stick to my curfew and be obedient to my foster carers.

My experience of being in foster care is not a bad one. I do feel extremely privileged when I hear of bad experiences of being in care. It was part of Gods story for my life that it would be through the care system God would reach out and save me.

At church we would have travelling guest speakers and I would frequently get called up to the front and have words of prophecy spoken over me, and they would tell me things concerning Gods plans for my life. Whenever these words were spoken over me, all I ever could see was the vision of the thousands of people listening to my story. These words sparked such hope and dreams for my future. I always knew God had big plans for me. You just feel it deep within. I knew God didn't spare my lifeless soul on that hospital bed for no reason. The first ever scripture I learnt was:

"For I know the plans I have for you says the Lord. Plans to give you a hope and a future" Jeremiah 29:11

This scripture always gave me peace and hope to know that things would and could only get better, it empowered me to dream big and made me want to be the best me that I could be.

Although my then current circumstances weren't ideal; I was a foster child, I didn't live with my real family and my upbringing was one I was embarrassed of. God still loved me and accepted me. He still wanted to use me. I knew God had a plan for my life and that one day He was going to use me to share my story to hundreds of people.

The only issue was, it was easy to hope for the future. I still was living away from my family and continued to have inward insecurities that were left untreated.

I began feeling restless and wanted my own independence. I was wishing years away, wanting to be old enough to live on my own to have a place of my own.

CHAPTER
9

Back Home

One month after my overdose my mum had given birth to a baby girl, my sister. I had always visited my sister as much as possible. Becoming a big sister to her was giving her something that I never had. I was hurt that I was not living at home to be more present in my sister's life. It made me resentful towards my mother. I was too young to understand the implications and my mum's inabilities to care for me as an adolescent.

Facing the rejection from my biological family left me insecure regarding my foster family. My lack of self-esteem didn't allow me to feel entirely part of the family with my carers. Like any young person, I missed my home and wanted to be a part of what I knew as *'family'*. Knowing I had a baby sister of my own made me feel as though it was somewhere, I felt needed and wanted. I had spent my entire life an only child. Therefore, the desire to want to go back home to my birth family grew stronger. It had built up to the point that I felt so hurt and alone. I knew I was not a biological member of my Foster Families' home and over time I allowed my insecurities to get the better of me. After two years of being placed into Foster Care, I left my foster home and ran away to be back with my mum and sister

I wanted to try and be a part of my family again. I thought I could mimic my foster family into my real family – something that would never happen. I moved my belongings back in to my mum's house, although my room was now entirely emptied and rearranged. I slept on the floor and tried to complete my last month of school before the summer holidays. I knew I had made the wrong decision to run away from my foster care placement; I was back to what I had initially tried to escape.

I thought moving back home would have felt better. I was wrong. It was as if I was a lodger, a stranger. I would come home from school, stay in my room and leave the next morning. It was challenging. Moving back to my mums meant my usual commute of 30 minutes to school would now take me just short of 2 hours. One month after moving in, my summer holidays began.

August 2007   *Names have been changed to protect the privacy of individuals

I had gone on a two-week holiday with my mum and baby sister. While we were away, my step-dad was looking after my mum's house, it also was his birthday. Kelly*, a childhood friend of mums came to visit not knowing we were out of the country. Not wanting to turn her away my stepdad invited her back that evening to celebrate his birthday with a few friends. Kelly later returned with one of her daughters Tyra*, who alike was my childhood friend. Sadly, that night would end terribly.

The week following his birthday my mum and I returned from our holiday. Having enjoyed quality time together, we were refreshed, tanned and well rested.

Upon landing, to our surprise her partner was waiting at the airport. I planned a taxi for us to get back home already. My mum was shocked, thinking it was a nice gesture that he had come to collect her. However, the mood soon changed from excitement to worry once my step-dad ran up to her and said: *"I need to talk to you, urgently"*. He told me to make my way with the taxi and they will be there soon.

I arrive back home after a few hours, and as I walked into the front room, he gets up to leave. *"I'm on bail"* he whispers as he walks out. Provokingly, he said that to get a response, although I shrugged it off not wanting to show my interest. Of course, I was wanting to know exactly what had happened. I take a seat on the sofa and look at my mum as she's sitting there in utter silence. Given his past, I felt deep down I knew it was something horrible. The silence in the house was morbid, as if someone had died. My mother asked a friend to come over, to have someone by her side to try and explain to me, what had happened.

Finally, it is explained to me. On the night of his birthday, Kelly came to visit with Tyra. My step-dad invited them to come over to celebrate his birthday. There was a handful of other people, so Kelly agreed. She had bought Tyra who could sleep in my room, as it was spare. It would be during the night as she slept. She would wake up with my step-dad making unwanted sexual advances towards her.

Immediately, she screamed for her mum, the police would be called, and he would be arrested and charged for the attempted rape of a minor. As I heard the story unfold, the story creating pictures in my mind, I snap out of my daydream and realise it was in my mum's house. Reality hits me, *"My bedroom?"* I shout! This horrible ordeal had taken place in the room I had grown up in.

"My best friend's sister?!", "Why did he have to taint a friend of mine?" She was so traumatised she had to undergo serious counselling and therapy for years following. Most of all I felt so angry that again my mum was acting as nothing had happened. *"Why are you allowing him to be here?"* I shouted. Again, I was too young to understand my mother's coping mechanism was to clam up, be withdrawn and distant. I wanted to scream and shout and get angry to tell my mum how silly she was to be with such a person. I couldn't get angry with her, I felt so let down. I was so disappointed. I had left foster care and come *back home* to this? My mum was worth so much more than to be with such a person! I felt like I was the mother, and she was the daughter. All those feelings I had felt when I was younger came flooding back in. Something I had tried to run away from, yet I was stuck again. This time though self-harm and suicide couldn't come into my thinking. I knew my life had been spared. I knew God had plans for me, and that I was going somewhere in life. My mum's house carried way too many traumatic memories. It was a place that

I needed to escape from and never come back to. The very same night I couldn't step foot in my bedroom. I tried to sleep in my mum's room, but the thought of what happened disgusted me. I just could not sleep at all – How could I sleep? I felt so dirty and couldn't stop crying. I lay there, unable to get the thoughts out my mind of what had happened! I hear my mother snoring; this confirmed to me that she had peacefully fallen asleep. It seemed this incident had not at all caused her any upset?

After a few hours, around 1 am I quietly gathered a few clothes, leaving my mum a note saying I couldn't stay there anymore and ran away. I left home – Never to live there again.

It would be the following year that my stepfather would be charged and sentenced to imprisonment for the attempted rape of my friend. This second accusation now finally resulting in an imprisonment had become the chance for my mum to end her relationship, leave this man and to get on with her life and focus on my sister and myself; her children. I sat her down and told her what I wanted her to do. I said that this could be the time that we could build a healthier mother and daughter bond, that I would support her no matter what and most importantly help her with my sister. She just couldn't. She had been a single mother with me for over 10 years. She couldn't bear the thought of being abandoned by a man again. I pitied her for her lack of strength, knowing this was what he deserved and that he was in the wrong, he had to face the repercussions. It was as if my mother was a young teenager going through heartache and I was the mother. I had never seen my mum cry. She hadn't cried when I overdosed. She hadn't cried when I went into Foster Care. There was my mother, now crying.

After running away that night, I struggled for the next couple of years to find anywhere to settle. I slept at a few friends' houses until it was inconvenient. In this time, I still tried to complete my final year of High School to pass my GCSE's. No one knew what I was going through.

A year later I declared myself homeless and I had begun living in a YMCA hostel. I remember this being such a lonely and challenging period of my life.

It got so severe that I would wake up in the mornings and the first thing I would do was get high. I would be high, and this would help me numb my feelings of hunger and numb my emotions. I had been so negatively impacted by my step dad's attack on my friend. It was so severe it was as if I was the victim. It sent me into a downward spiral. I lost a huge amount of weight; the lowest weight saw me wearing UK size 4 clothing. People would comment about how much weight I had lost and always be adamant that they needed to feed me. Something people did not know was that behind closed doors I had fallen into drug addiction and started smoking drugs daily, and it wasn't long before I was heavily addicted.

My friends were all moving on to college and sixth form. My whole life crumbled that previous summer when my friend was assaulted. It sent me into a dark depression. I couldn't find the motivation for education – I dropped out from school rejecting my acceptance into colleges and sixth forms. I felt like a failure, all my friends were enjoying student life and living their innocent lives. Whilst I on the other hand already had to live independently and fend for myself. I was too insecure and felt I wouldn't succeed at anything. All my hopes, dreams and aspirations were tarnished, and I felt helpless.

By this point, I was now 16 years old, and for the next two years I would isolate myself, not maintaining many relationships. I stopped going to church because I was embarrassed that I had made such a wrong choice running away from Foster Care.

After all, my carers were the Pastors. I thought people at church would judge me. Being without my friends, and church community was lonely and isolating.

Although I had left the care system, now facing drug addiction and was alone, God still had a plan for my life.

CHAPTER

10

Arms of My Father

fter two years, I turned 18. My friends were beginning University and I would see Facebook posts of how happy they were. It had been two years and I had done nothing fruitful with my life apart from a part-time waitressing job. This begun re-building my confidence. Enough for me to start looking for a full-time job to help me have a career. Having already embarked into the working world, I started to think that there had to be more to my story than this! I knew God was there and that He loved me. Although I felt so distant from Him, I had done so much wrong and I was a hypocrite of a Christian. I knew God spared my life for a great future. Even in my hostel I would tell people about Jesus, most of our talks would be over our drug taking.

This hypocrisy led to me picking up my Bible again, and I would begin reading more. I soon started talking more and more to God again. Even when I was high, God soon helped me cut down on my drug taking. After a while, my confidence began to build up again. I began wanting to do more with my life. I started to think either I continue this path and become a nobody in life. Or I get my act together find a full-time job/ get back into education. From that moment I decided enough was enough and once I had made that conscious decision to change God met me where I was at in that stage of life, once again. The next day I woke up and instead of getting high by smoking drugs. I chose to pray, read my bible, and get out into the world. As I walked out of the hostel, I had no idea where I would go or what I would do? As I walked through my local town, I saw a careers advisor's centre. I walked in and spoke with a worker saying I wanted to get into work. We spoke through some opportunities and together we filled in job applications. I asked God to give me the right job and He answered my prayer! - I had an interview for the very next day.

Two days after that, I was confirmed as successful for the position and was to start three days after that! Getting a full-time job helped me build my confidence and begin to have something to focus my time and attention on. I began praying about moving out of the hostel and soon enough I moved into my very own flat. Everything was falling into place and going well for me. I was now 19 and it had been four years that I had stopped going to church. Simply, from the embarrassment of leaving foster care. I decided to go back. I still loved Jesus and wanted Him more than ever and was willing to live however was needed to have Him back, regardless of what people thought of me.

I had been reading the Parable of the Lost Son. It was talking about me, I was the lost daughter! I didn't realise I was coming back to the Father's House when I rededicated my life to Jesus. It was only a few weeks after I felt it was shown to me as I read my Bible. The passage spoke of a child who after having taken his inheritance from his father, before his Dad had passed away! Squandered the money with what was likened to modern day gambling, nights out, designer clothes, and prostitutes. Once the son had 'lived the dream' he had a reality check once all the money ran out. He tried to get a job working for minimum wage. During this time, he remembered his dad who was wealthy and that he had all the son ever needed. He then decided he would humbly return home, say sorry and work for his dad to make up for the wrong he had done. It was as he was making his way back to his Father's house, and when he was in the distance he was spotted by his Father *"So he returned home to his father. And while he was still a long way off, his father saw him coming. Filled with love and compassion, he ran to his son, embraced him and kissed him" Luke 15:20 [NLT version]*. Although I had messed up, time and time again. God forgave me and was happy to have me home, I ran in to *the arms of my Father*! My church family were so happy to see me, no one even knew I had left foster care. I re-dedicated my life to Jesus and asked God forgive me for being distant from Him. I asked Him to heal me from my addiction to marijuana. I felt God give me the strength to throw out all my drugs and delete any contacts I had that would be of a bad influence. I have never taken drugs since! I still faced one addiction though – smoking cigarettes. I was that person who would always make sure I was well out of any church member's view. Then once I had left a service I would begin to smoke. A few month's following God would heal me from my addiction to cigarettes. One evening I was at church, and a speaker shared about a man who was healed of his addiction to cigarettes, in that moment the speaker looked directly at me. It was as if he knew I smoked, how could he? He didn't know me. I felt the conviction of God towards smoking for the first time in my life. I had never felt smoking cigarettes was wrong until that day. My heart was beating fast, not of embarrassment or guilt, but it felt so purifying! There in the service as the speaker continued preaching, I quietly said under my breath, *"Ok God I'm going to quit"*! That evening as I left the church, I did what I had always done. I walked a few yards from the church and when I was well out of view from anyone who was from the church. I reached into my pocket for a cigarette and began to smoke. Only this time - it was different. It tasted disgusting! I tried another cigarette just encase this one was faulty. Again, the taste was foul. This had never, ever happened before. I had been smoking for five years by this point. In that moment I was reminded of the conversation I had with God in the service I had just left. As I recalled the conversation it was highlighted to me speaking about my own strength, *"I will quit"*, 'I', meaning in **my** will-power, **my own strength**. Will-power was not going to help break this addiction. This time, I looked up at the orange hazed light, polluted evening London sky and said: *"Ok, God you and **all** of Heaven and even all your Heavenly angels are going to have to help me on this one because I can't do it on my own"*. I put my hand in my pocket scrunched the box of cigarettes, marched to the nearest bin and threw them away. I haven't touched or desired a cigarette ever since!

CHAPTER

11

Fulfilling Destiny

As time progressed I was reading more of God's word and allowing it to transform my life entirely. I started seeing so much change in my life. Change for the better! Now 20 years old, I prayed for a new job, and God gave me a new job. A position which I wasn't qualified for and a salary that was seven years beyond what the average person my age was earning.

I began asking God what His will was for my life. I was challenged by my Pastor when he was preaching one Sunday, saying if you want to know what God's will is for your life, serve! So, I did. I had begun serving in our Youth Ministry as a Youth Leader, I became a teacher in Sunday School as well as enrolling at Bible School. Bible School would serve as a training field where I would become teachable, mouldable and fully equipped for the ministry (vocation) that lay before me.

September 2011

September 2011, during my first term of Bible School, I had received teaching on fasting. I thought I would take the following day off work and give fasting a go. From here I would begin hearing God.

As I began, I watched a movie on Mother Theresa's life. After some time in prayer and being challenged by her sacrificial life, I felt a strong desire for the country of Albania and wanted to somehow volunteer in an orphanage. I felt God was speaking to me and putting the desire on my heart. At that time, I didn't know how, when or where. However, I started telling people I was going to go to Albania.

February 2012

I felt so close to God I decided to get baptised. In this time, I had repetitive dreams of me with my future spouse marching through the streets of London with thousands of young people following us. On the day of my baptism, as I am lifted out of the water from the baptismal pool, barely able to stand one of the elders Pastor Danny shared a vision with me.

To my surprise, he said that he saw me and a young male (my future husband) with fire all around us leading thousands of young people to Jesus. I more earnestly began praying into getting married and praying for my future husband.

Having fasted in September 2011 and being able to hear the voice of God. This prepared me for a few months later when God would speak to me to tell me to go on a Daniel Fast for ten days, in April 2012.

April 2012

This was the first time I felt God speak to me regarding a fast. I had never done a Daniel Fast before, but I knew God had spoken to me. *What was this fast for*? I wondered, but I did not know. God knew. During this time of fasting. Something happened. It was during April 2012, God had woken me up consecutively in the early hours, for two weeks to pray. Each time I would wake up, I would ask God what He wanted me to pray about, He would only press on my heart: "*Pray for your husband*", "*Husband? What husband?*". To which I felt a response with such urgency: "*Just pray*"

I would pray my usual prayer "*God, I pray for my husband right now, wherever he is. If he is not saved Lord yet, I pray for his salvation. Keep him safe and help him draw near to you. Help us to wait for each other. In your perfect timing align our paths to meet*". It wasn't a long prayer, but I felt peace and went back to sleep. It would happen repetitively over the next two weeks, so I knew God was using this *fast* towards my future marriage.

Unknown to me, my *now* husband Daniel would at that time be finding out the outcome of a court case, which could have seen him imprisoned for eight years for a kidnapping charge! It was during those two weeks; the case would be withdrawn from court, **and he would end up surrendering his life to Jesus** in that exact month.

Bearing in mind, we were not going to meet for another 15 months in the future. That is supernatural!

June 2012

A few months later, nine months to the date of when I first tried fasting and God had spoken to me about the Nation of Albania. In June 2012 I embarked on my first mission trip to a town called Korce in Albania!

When God had initially laid Albania on my heart, people thought I was crazy, or that it was a faze but I knew I'd be going. As time progressed, I would eventually meet a group of Christians who regularly served as Missionaries in Albania and I joined them to help serve in an orphanage, girls safe house and church between June and July in 2012.

November 2012

I now had been serving in church in our Youth Ministry for nearing two years, teaching in the Sunday School and was studying my final year at the Bible School. However, something still wasn't quite fulfilling me on the inside. I had been so busy in the church, I practically lived at church.

Monday and Tuesdays were Bible School, Wednesday was Youth Discipleship, Thursdays – Prayer Meeting, One Friday a month – all night prayer meetings, Saturday – Evangelism, and Sundays consisted of either teaching in the Sunday school or the evening Youth Service. All whilst holding down a full-time 9-5 job.

Our youth weren't very interested and did not show much enthusiasm or passion for Jesus. As a teenager I had grown up in church hearing about revival, miracles, signs and wonders. But I didn't see power demonstrated within our churches. The same move of God that I encountered when I was thirteen seemed forgotten. Our church members were reducing, the young people were slowly losing interest.

By the end of 2012, I felt that I needed to be around like-minded Christians and exploit my passion in a different place. I spent New Year's at my church but was so annoyed that it was yet *'another church service'*. I knew there was more to God than the four walls of the church. I vowed that next year (2013) I would not be spending it at my church!

January 2013

From January 2013 I decided to step down from serving in ministry as I felt I was giving out from a dry place. I wasn't as fired up and raring to go as I was when I came back to church in May 2011. There wasn't much enthusiasm for the young people, most of them had fallen away, and back to their lives before they knew Christ. It always seemed you had to have been a Christian for a stone age before you could be recognised or even qualified to be used by Him. Rarely were the young people given opportunity to share the passion that was burning within their hearts; which was quenching the fire.

I was holding down a good job in Central London, on a decent salary, with my own flat, car and independence. However, it wasn't long until I started to feel empty again. I was basing a lot of my success and happiness on what I had achieved to show people how well I was doing. Yet, I still lacked on the inside. On the outside, I was doing everything right, but I knew from within there had to be more!

I was lonely. I didn't have much family and wanted a family of my own. I wanted to meet someone who I could do life with. Not knowing my biological father had implications on my spiritual relationship with my Heavenly Father. As much as I was on fire for

Jesus, I hadn't encountered God as a dad. I had never had a father so was unable to understand what it meant to have a good father. I would begin to ask God to reveal Himself to me as daddy and allow myself to receive His love as a daughter. During this time, I would read of radical encounters in the Bible of the early church.

I held dearly to all the promises and prophetic words I had from God; that I would be a preacher and travel the nations sharing my story.

The more I was seeking God the more restless I was becoming in church. I just knew there was more to Christianity than what I experienced for 3 hours on a Sunday morning. There was a lifestyle of the supernatural that I had only heard of but not experienced. As weeks passed, I felt like I no longer fitted in and no one understood what frustrations I had. They were content with gossiping during the week, then putting on their finest clothes and sitting on their seat's week in and week out but not seeing any change in their day-to-day lives. We were playing church!

I asked God to guide me through this challenging season of my life even though I didn't understand what was happening. I leaned on Him and trusted it would all work out. I decided to start visiting other churches and going to Christian events, all in my quest to find God and His power. *I needed to fulfil my destiny!* I needed to find somewhere where I could be understood. Maybe I could find somewhere to fit in, somewhere my calling could be recognised and nurtured. Nonetheless, I would continue my final months to complete my studies at Bible School.

April 2013

Prayers for my future husband continued and one night in April 2013 as I was sleeping, God spoke to me. (**One year** to the date when God first spoke to me to fast and pray)

My prayer again was simple:

"If he wasn't saved yet – that he'd come to know Jesus. Wherever he was to keep him safe. Help him to wait for me as I wait for him. To align our paths in His perfect timing."

This time, however, God showed me a dream, but it was like an open vision. I hear from God regularly but still to this day, I have never heard God so specifically. He told me how I would meet my husband and the details entailing our ministry;

God showed me my husband to-be was already in his ministry and that he was an Evangelist. That I would meet him outside of my church, come alongside him and be a strong support system to him behind the scenes of ministry. It would be internationally that together we would travel the world and serve the Lord, preaching the gospel of Jesus Christ.

I was very excited about my dream, and I wrote it down, interpreted it. Prayed over it and shared it with a few of my close friends.

DREAM OF DANIEL

"I was walking out of my church with Jesus by my side. As we walked outside, I saw a huge and very long coach but more like a blacked-out tour bus, bigger than I've seen. Jesus was walking with me every step of the way, and He reached out His hand for me to hold as He led me to get on the bus. There was no one else around. I got on the coach walked right to the back to the far corner. There was a young man. He was waiting for me. I went and sat next to him as I went next to him, he laid his head on my lap as if to take a nap. I was there for him as a support. The man in my dream, his hand was waved in front of me as if Jesus was making a point for me to look at his hand. I said to Jesus "he's supposed to be married", the man's hand was waved in front of me again. Again, I said "Jesus, he is supposed to be married" it happened again and for the third time after this repetitive dialogue.
I said, "Is this, my husband?"

CHAPTER

12

Finding The One

"Seek first the kingdom of God, and His righteousness and all these things shall be added unto you" Matthew 6:33

One month later, May 2013. As my pursuit for the things of God continued. I began stepping more into what God planned for me, and I was starting to experience the supernatural.

In my quest to find God, I would prayerfully seek which church to visit each week. One week he led me to a church in West London, and as the Pastor was preaching, I felt the presence of God so strong. As he made an altar call, he said: *"There is someone here, and you can feel heat all over your hands, come forward if that's you"*.

That was me my hands were literally burning. I ran so fast to the front, he reached out his arms and whoosh, I hit the ground so fast like a sack of potatoes. He prayed over me and said *"There is heat from your hands. When you feel that heat, you will lay hands on people, they are going to begin to get healed"*.

The next day I began my final term of Bible School and was soon due to graduate within a few weeks. It was break time during seminars, and I was walking past a lady named Jean to go to get a drink and I gently laid my hand on her arm to walk past without startling her. Shortly after, as I am walking back to class, she came running towards me.

Jean rushes towards me and says in her strong Caribbean accent *"Where have you been, I was looking for you down the corridor, and I had to stop you?"*. She grabs my hands and just stares at them, *"Girl, I don't know what happened, but when you just touched me earlier, I felt heat all go through me body!"* I was in awe! That is what happened when I visited the church God told me to the morning before. She took my hot drink and carefully put it to the side. She grabbed my hands, and said: *"Girl, you gotta lay those hands on me again, me been having too much pain and I know God is gonna heal me"*.

I laid hands on her and commanded that pain to leave her body. At that moment I could feel that heat again burning on my hands and the power of God was penetrating her body. She felt so much better throughout the rest of our course.

Ready to complete my last term of Bible School, my graduation was approaching. I was so hungry for God. I was eager to know now more than ever what I would do after I finish Bible School. I knew I was in preparation for ministry.

Jean's healing encouraged me so much, I began more confidently sharing the gospel with people, this time I began asking people if I could pray for their healing. One day as I was at a London underground station, I encountered 4 men with speech impediments. I shared the gospel with them and prayed for them too! This was the beginning of something new.

June 2013

This would be the second time I felt God tell me to go on a Daniel Fast. This time for 21 days. This fast would begin on Sunday 2nd June 2013 and end Sunday 23rd June 2013.

During the fast I got a phone call from my friend Shanna, she said a lady that I had once prayed for had bought tickets for us to both attend an upcoming meeting, at Kensington Temple in London. I felt very thankful that this woman remembered me enough and had gone out of her way to pay for me to go. The day came to attend this meeting. It just so happened it coincided with the final day of my Daniel Fast.

Saturday 22nd June 2013

I picked up Shanna from her workplace and as we were driving to Kensington Temple, she mentions she needs to eat. Seeing as we arrived early, we walked to seek out food spots. I was very hungry and now excited that it was the last day of my fast. Shanna opts for a good-looking pizza, I settled for a small piece of fruit and a hot water as the Daniel Fast permitted.

As we sat in my car killing time before the service began, we had a good catch up. Shanna confides in me saying she had met a Christian and he felt she was his wife. She was a friend who had no desire to ever be married. She loved Jesus so much she wanted to be married to Him forever. Celibate like Paul, she wasn't interested in a man, and she didn't know what to do. He had wanted to take her out. I was so shocked by this news, and quickly irritable (partly due to the fact I hadn't eaten anything reasonable for 21 days now!). I snapped and told her to just go on a date. What harm could it be, he was Christian, after all.

My flesh got the better of me at that moment, and as I sat in the driver's seat of my car, I said to myself, *"what about me? I haven't met anyone yet. I've been praying for years, plus she's not even desiring to get married, and she's possibly already met her husband"*.

We then walk into the church, Kensington Temple, London and are greeted by Shanna's friend Rita. This is the kind lady who had purchased a ticket for me to be able to attend this meeting. Rita then walks us to our seats, which she has already reserved. As I walk through the door, I could see Daniel through the glass door approaching from the other side, and he opens the door for me Rita goes on to introduce us saying she had invited Daniel, as well as several others. We briefly say hello and take our seats.

Feeling bad for my inward attitude and jealousy towards Shanna's new interest from her male friend, I suddenly remembered I had left my bible in my car and tell Shanna *"I've forgotten my Bible, I'll be right back"*.

I was so irritable and now feeling heavy. Therefore, I took advantage of some time alone to pray to God and regain my peace. Sitting in my car, I vented to God about the disgust with my attitude, feeling so sorry for myself. I felt as though this revealed that I was a horrible person. After all, I would always want to be celebrating for a sister. Not resentful. I was supposed to be a Christian! I was in a season of fasting, going through a time of consecration, trying to rid myself of any impurities in my heart.

I went on to tell God;

"God, I don't mean to feel like this, but she practically doesn't even want to get married, and she has someone interested in her, and there's me waiting for the 'one', and I haven't even met him yet! I need to go in and feel right with you. I'm sorry for feeling like this I'm just tired and looking forward to eating. Please help me to remain right in my heart, and I thank you that our paths will be aligned with the right timing".

So, I said my usual prayer as I leave my car:

> *"God wherever he is, keep him safe.*
> *If he doesn't know you may he come to know you.*
> *In your perfect timing, it will happen!"*

I rushed to close my prayer and left my car.

Knowing I was so much more mature than this, I put it down to being hungry, and hormonal. I felt a lot better and knew that God forgave me, so I sensed that I shouldn't beat myself up so much about it! Unbeknown to me, my future husband was inside that very church, and sitting right in front of me!

I make my way back to the church not entirely in the right place. I knew I had to forgive myself. I chose to push through and try to focus on God and the service.

So far, throughout worship I'm just having a massive inward battle, trying to feel right with God. I had my hands in the air worshipping, but on the inside, I just knew my heart wasn't in the right place. I begin to have this argument with God. Again, repeating, squinting my eyes with my hands raised: "*I know you have someone for me and I'm sorry for feeling like this, please help me to concentrate on you*".

I genuinely was so hungry by this point I knew my patience was running low, and this made me feel a lot better now that I had let my frustration's out. Thankfully, though, there wasn't any preaching that day. I think the enemy had condemned me so much. I wouldn't have been able to focus. Therefore, it was nice when the guy on the pulpit said he felt the presence of God so strong that we should turn and pray for those around us. Praying for others helped me take my eyes off myself and focus on God. I go off to pray for a woman, I close my eyes, and I hear someone is also praying for her.

As I open my eyes, who else decided to pray for her?

Daniel. Daniel is on the other side, praying for this woman's blind eye to open! The service closed, I mingled and socialised. Then I briefly spoke to Daniel. I didn't think much of that night and went home.

A few days later I invited Shanna over to my apartment. I just had to be honest with her, be truthful, and tell her how I reacted and why I reacted so wrongly. I was so repentant of my attitude towards her and confessed how I had felt insecure about hearing her news, and that it wasn't anything personal. I was happy though, as it was exposed and given to God in prayer. Of course, I too wanted to meet someone. She thanked me for being honest and was so gracious and empathetic. We had a good hug and prayed in agreement that it would happen for me too, in God's perfect timing.

July 2013

A few weeks later, I received an invitation to join a gathering in London of young Christians on fire for Jesus that met every Monday. I felt to go along and visit. After all, I was in a season where I had left my church to find God. I asked God if I should go. I believed this was the next step. But the meetings were in Elephant and Castle, in South London, and I lived in West London – it was just too far. Within that split second. I said: *"God if it's in Elephant and Castle, I'm not going. If it were closer, I would go"*.

Exactly one minute later, I get an additional message from a member of the group saying, *"By the way, they recently changed the location and moved to Central London, I feel you need to be there"*. I just knew it was God, and I went. Going to this event would be where I would meet Daniel for the second time. After meeting for that second time we connected very briefly. The following week would be the third time we met and would talk. This time we had a more in-depth conversation, it was an instant connection. Effortlessly we conversed, had so much in common and continued our friendship over text. The month's following Daniel and I would get to know each other more over texting. We would meet up for the first time two months later to evangelise. Daniel considered this a date, I was totally oblivious!

September 2013

The following month (3 months after initially meeting) God spoke to me and showed me that Daniel was my spouse whom I would marry. We spoke that night and we both shared that we believed there was more to our friendship in God's eyes and began dating. Knowing one day we would marry.

Sunday 2nd March 2014

Six months later. Daniel was invited to minister at the church which I had grown up in, where my foster parents pastored. He preached and did an altar call and the fire of God was falling over young and old.

As the service was ending, Daniel called me, my friends to the front. Thinking he wanted to take a picture to honour preaching in my home church with our friends and family. As he began talking, I see him reach into his pocket and before I knew it; he was kneeling on the floor asking for my hand in marriage!

In shock, I did not know where to look. An eruption of clapping, cheering and gasps filled the room.

I said "*Yes!*".

It was a beautiful moment and I found it even more special that Daniel had been so honourable to do it before my church family who had known my story and helped shepherd and guide me in my walk from when I joined them as a young, suicidal, thirteen-year-old teenager, now to a young adult embarking on marriage. Nine months later we married on Saturday 15th November 2014 and on Sunday 5th June two years later in 2016 we welcomed our first daughter Zarah Martha Chand. Together as a family we are now serving God full-time, travelling the world, sharing our stories with people we meet; helping change lives and lead people home into the loving arms of Jesus.

CHAPTER

13

Daniel's Perspective

I asked Daniel to share his perspective on how we met

I needed my wife. I was in ministry, and sometimes it would get lonely. One day I prayed to God, and I asked Him *"Father I do not just want a 'Christian' wife but somebody who is on fire for you!"* I was particular; I described long, dark hair, olive skin, and beautiful hands. She had to be on fire! I remember sharing this with my mum and we prayed together.

A few weeks after I had prayed this, Rita, the same person had invited me to the exact event on Saturday 22nd June 2013 that Tanya was also going to be attending. At that time, I did not know her and was not aware that she had been asked to come. I remember meeting Tanya at the door briefly. But it was during worship that Tanya caught my attention. For some reason, I quickly looked behind me. As I saw Tanya, she was passionately worshipping. I then heard the Holy Spirit say, *"Imagine that being your wife"*. Then I thought this is a distraction, so I bought my focus back to the worship.

The preacher then asked the congregation to pray for one another. Tanya and I ended up praying for the same woman. Afterwards, we began to speak, very briefly. That was it, and we had exchanged numbers primarily for networking reasons.

A couple of weeks later we would meet again at a different meeting in Central London. That was so God ordained, given we probably never would have seen each other again. I knew some of our mutual friends could have invited her to this meeting, so I was hoping she would be there, and she was!

The second time we met we didn't say much apart from "*bye*" as we left. Fortunately, the next week I was due to preach there and this time I was hoping she would be there again, so I could impress her with my preaching.

That following week, we met again, except this time I made sure I stopped her to talk more. The moment we began to speak, fireworks went off! We immediately clicked. It was destiny, and I knew that she was my wife.

That summer we would go on to become best friends. Months later, after finishing preaching in her home church, I called her to the front and got down on one knee in front of all her friends and church family and asked her to marry me.

I'm glad she said, "*Yes*"!

CHAPTER

14

A Reason To Live

In my heart, I had always been so grateful to God for sparing my life, that in return I said *"God, all I can do is give my life solely for your purposes. Just give me a loving husband, a family of my own and I will give it all to you"*.

God is so faithful in His promises; His plans are always bigger than our human-made ideas. I asked for a husband, He blessed me with a partner that I could do life with and together we would live to serve Jesus and expand His Kingdom on the earth. I asked him for a family, he gave me an adopted heavenly family and a child of my own.

Sharing the love of Jesus and the Heart of the Father is my passion.

I grew up facing rejection, loneliness and instability. I tried to take my own life at the tender age of 13. My life has now changed for the better. I am so thankful, to now be married, be a mother and now am an advocate for life!

I have not once thought of taking my own life since and have been healed from all emotional and physical scars from my childhood and past.

Through Jesus Christ I now have *a reason to live!*

Reconciliation

To this day, my mum and I have been able to restore our relationship. I give God all the glory for it. As I have grown, I have allowed God to heal me of my life's hurts and pain. I have forgiven my mum, and I love her with genuine love. She didn't know any better, and she tried her best. She has had her hurts in life, and I have grown to accept that. She isn't a bad person. She has just made a few bad choices. The fact that Jesus came into my life, I can now use my story to empower and help save others – I am happy to use the bad things that happened to me to relate to others and lead them home to Jesus.

My story was part of God's plan, He uses what was intended for bad for good.

As any person regardless of how bad your parents may be, they'll always be your parents, and you'll want to do your best to help.

I thank God for His mercy towards me because I am not perfect. Therefore, allowing me to show my mum mercy in return. To this day, my mum now visits a church, and I believe God for her Salvation.

CHAPTER

15

The Father's Heart

Fatherlessness causes a lot of our society's problems. Due to broken down family relationships. Generation after generation, hurting children go into the world hurting others. It is God's desire that He be a Father to His children. He wants us as sons and daughters to know that we are loved and to share this same love to the world and bring as many of His children back home to Him.

God showed the world how much he loves humanity by sending His son, Jesus into the world as a sacrifice for all the wrong we have and will ever do. Jesus was nailed to a cross, the weight of the world's sin upon God's sacrifice. Whether you accept it or not, Jesus paid the penalty for sin, which is eternal damnation in hell. Making a way for us to enter Heaven and live forever in Gods kingdom.

I may not have known my earthly father, but I know my Heavenly Father. I was suicidal, now I am loved, accepted and living with purpose.

It is *the Father's heart* that He not only is known to you as God but that you also allow God to become **your Father**, your Daddy. You may not have had a dad growing up. Maybe the father you did have wasn't always there for you or the best role model. God can be both the mother and father that you haven't had. It doesn't matter how far you have been away without Him, or how hurt you have been from life's ordeals. If you allow Jesus into your heart, He can heal every wound, emotional scar, and pain in an instant.

I pray that this book has given you hope and inspiration to not give up or let go of your dreams.

Like me, you may not have had a good start in life, but it's not about what you've come from, but it's about discovering the plan God has for you and going on to have a better quality of life for yourself, your family and your loved ones.

Most importantly it is about making sure your loved ones know about Heaven and how to get there.

You are a product of your choices, and one of the best decisions you could ever make is to say "*Yes*" to Jesus

God works all things together for our good, and I found my hope and peace through Jesus Christ. Jesus is our hope in a hopeless world [*Romans 8:28*]

I share my story to help others

You can too...

The Meaning of Life

I am now really enjoying life. Knowing I have a reason to live, gives me joy. A joy only found in Jesus Christ. I get hard days, and I'm not immune from the issues of life, the difference now though is that I have a joy that can never be taken from me. Through Jesus, Prayer and Meditation I can go through anything.

I have gone on to share my testimony in different parts of the world, in churches and even with people I meet on streets, in coffee shops and even in a toilet! I have now written this book, as a way of sharing what Jesus has done for me. I could keep this a secret; however, God has done tremendous things for me and in my life, and I cannot keep quiet.

To have a father and a family of my own, this is something that I desired ever since I was a young girl.

This desire was there from the very beginning. When God created the world, He then made Adam in the garden of Eden and said, *"everything was perfect"*. Even in that perfection, God still said it is not good for man to be alone.

From the very beginning of Gods plan, He created us to be relational and intimate beings, created for relationship. The desire to love and want love is from Him. When a person knows their death is imminent, they don't ask to be held by their money or their possessions, they long to be surrounded by their loved ones - people.

When God created us, He mirrored us in His likeness. It is these very passions that resemble our God-like nature, a desire from our Heavenly Father.

It says in 1 John 3 that we are called children of God. He wants us to become His children. Will you allow Him to become your Father? People take out home contents insurance, phone insurance, car insurance if the worst were to happen. Have you prepared your eternal insurance? Do you know what will happen when your body ceases, and your spirit leaves this earthen vessel? It says in the book of Ecclesiastes, there is a time to be born and a time to die.

In the same way, you were physically born into your earthly family on the day of entering this world. There is a point in your life when you must become born again, into a new family - the family of God. A moment in eternity when you are adopted into the family of God and reconciled to your Heavenly Father, Daddy God. You must be Spiritually born again to become a child of God - By accepting Jesus as your Lord and Saviour.

From that day your name is written in the Book of Life, [Revelation 21:27, Revelation 20:15, Luke 10:20], this is the book which is used to determine who goes to Heaven. How can your name be found in The Book of Life you may ask?

The moment a human being opens their heart to Jesus and believes He died on the Cross for their sins. Confesses they need forgiveness and asks Him into their life. At that moment ALL of Heaven and the Heavenly hosts rejoice, read Luke 15:7; they have the most amazing party, and that person's name becomes written in the Book of Life!

What a momentous time!

Today is your opportunity to be known by God and have your home prepared in Heaven.

Go and tell your loved ones, your friends. Wouldn't you want them to be with you for all of Eternity? It takes just one person to believe in you, one person to speak into your life and reveal who you were created to be and lead you home to the Father.

When you give your life to Jesus you become a part of Gods family! You are adopted by your Father God. If you have a good relationship with your earthly family that's great. If you don't well good news, you will have a new lineage, and you become a new person because of the blood of Jesus that washes you and forgives you of **all** wrong. You will be set free and redeemed from death and destruction.

Heaven will recognise your name. Your name will be written in the Book of Life, and you will have a certainty of where you will spend eternity.

A Fresh Start

If you are reading this and haven't given your life or opened your heart to Jesus, maybe you haven't lived your entire time on earth one hundred percent sold out for Christ, just say this prayer out loud:

———————————

Dear Jesus,

I've been living my life without you. I've been doing it in my strength. I've tried my way and look how far it has gotten me. I believe that you died on the cross in my place. That because of your wounds and beaten body at the Cross. I am healed and forgiven body, soul and Spirit. I ask you today to come into my life. Show me who you are and the way I should live. I want a relationship with you. I want to know God as my Father. Adopt me into your family. I open my heart to you right now, I want a new life, a life in Jesus. Heal me of all hurts, pain and addictions. Set me free from sin. Wash me clean in your precious blood.

From today I choose to live for you, have your way in my life.

Amen

Signed:

Name:

Date:

Contact

You may wish to pass this book to someone else who you feel will be encouraged by this story. If you have prayed and asked Jesus into your heart, let us know

Email: info@walkinglikejesus.org

Website: www.walkinglikejesus.org

OVERDOSE AT THE AGE OF 13

LIFE CHANGED AFTER I ATTEMPTED SUICIDE

Woman decided to follow foster parents to church

A LONDON woman is thanking God for the resurrection of Jesus after she recovered from being on a life support machine after taking a drug overdose.

Tanya Chand was just 13 when she attempted suicide – but after been taken in by Christian foster parents, she turned to God, is married and has now launched her own women's ministry.

Tanya, 22, told New Life: "I am overwhelmed by God's grace. I've done nothing to deserve the life I have now and that's the beauty of God. My dad left before I was born and I grew up with rejection and resenting my mother.

"I came to the conclusion my mother didn't really care and if I wasn't around nobody would notice. Just after my 13th birthday I decided to take an overdose and took over 100 pills. Reports show my mum put me in the shower to clean me up and put me to sleep, but I actually fell into a coma."

Tanya's mum rang the NHS the next day and the operator sent for an ambulance, which arrived with four police cars given the severity.

Tanya said: "Paramedics tried to revive me but there was no response. Upon arrival at hospital I was airlifted to central London intensive care unit and put on a life

support machine. I was lifeless in a coma and they were looking at turning the machines off. That's really where God stepped in."

While Tanya battled for her life, social services found her a foster home with Ian and Dennise Christensen, who are pastors at Wembley's New Life Christian Centre.

Dennise said: "Social services asked if we would take this girl who was on a life support machine. We pray about every referral and I wasn't going to take on a girl because I'd had a bad experience, but we prayed and I just felt that we should take her."

Remarkably, Tanya made a full recovery and remembers taking up Ian and Dennise's invite to church.

She added: "I visited a few times and at an altar call I said, 'God, if you're real, I want you to reveal yourself.' It was like I was given an entirely new life. I was washed clean of my past, I had a new family, new home and new life in Jesus."

Tanya, who married evangelist Daniel Chand last year, is using her experience to inspire others after establishing Eden's Masterpiece Women's Ministry.

"I remember praying, 'God, I really haven't had a good start, please give me a good husband so I can start my own family and raise godly children'," she said. "We're travelling Europe this year preaching, and it's amazing how God has turned my life around."

NEW START... Tanya Chand with her husband Daniel

Tanya at her wedding with foster parents Ian and Dennise Christensen